Home Office
Library & Den Design

Tina Skinner

Courtesy of Herman Miller, Inc.

Schiffer Publishing Ltd

4880 Lower Valley Road, Atglen, PA 19310 USA

Designed by John P. Cheek
Cover design by Bruce Waters
Type set in Americana/Lydian BT

ISBN: 0-7643-1842-X
Printed in China

Published by Schiffer Publishing Ltd.
4880 Lower Valley Road
Atglen, PA 19310
Phone: (610) 593-1777; Fax: (610) 593-2002
E-mail: Info@schifferbooks.com
Please visit our web site catalog at www.schifferbooks.com
We are always looking for people to write books on new and related subjects. If you have an idea for a book, please contact us at the above address.

This book may be purchased from the publisher.
Include $3.95 for shipping.
Please try your bookstore first.
You may write for a free catalog.

In Europe, Schiffer books are distributed by
Bushwood Books
6 Marksbury Avenue
Kew Gardens
Surrey TW9 4JF England
Phone: 44 (0) 20 8392 8585
Fax: 44 (0) 20 8392 9876
E-mail: Bushwd@aol.com
Free postage in the UK. Europe: air mail at cost.

Contents

Introduction 4
Corner Office 5
Against a Wall 13
Office Nooks 17
Minimalist 29
Flex Time 33
Conventional Workspaces 43
Unconventional 59
Reclaimed Spaces 63
Family Affairs 74
Executive Suites 80
Staying Connected 93
Locked Retreat 99
Contemporary 109
Classic Studies 127
All About Books 136
Resource Guide 143

Introduction

Be it a cubbyhole where you escape from family and phone to get work done, or a richly furnished, fire-lit room where you ask associates to gather – your work effectiveness is directly influenced by your environment. It may be important that your workplace emote power and prestige, that you have that high-backed leather swivel chair behind a massive oak desk. Or it may be a gathering place where brandy snifters are wielded and camaraderie encouraged. For many, an office is the all-important center of organization – where we try to keep the miscellaneous strings of our life neatly tied together. Working from home, with the aid of internet and fax, has become so easy that many people rarely need dress before heading off to work in the morning. Many new homes are built with a "bonus" room that serves as home office, and many an older home is undergoing remodeling to accommodate an office in the basement, spare bedroom, or even the garage. This book was conceived to help with the planning process. The goal is to help you visit many offices, from the comfort of your own, easily enabling you to choose colors, textures, and configurations that suit your tastes and needs. Even if you are working with a professional designer, this book gives you a launching point whereby design ideas can be pointed to. After all, when it comes to design, a picture truly is worth a thousand words.

Courtesy of Progress Lighting

Corner Office

Using every bit of possible space, a bookshelf was tucked under the console area, just beyond knee's reach.
Courtesy of Palliser® Furniture

Open shelves preserve the view, while tremendous storage options allow you to keep your desk looking orderly.
Courtesy of Offi

Simple pine furnishings make for an easily accessorized work area.
Courtesy of Palliser® Furniture

Clean, crisp white works well with all accessories. *Courtesy of The HON Company*

Maple and white work together in subtle tones for an L-shaped office space. *Courtesy of California Closets*

Modular units neatly configure for a clean,
L-shaped office area. *Courtesy of Palliser®
Furniture*

Below:
A home office also doubles as storage space
in a spare bedroom. Clean white cabinetry
discourages clutter. *Courtesy of Decorá*

A window within the office unit provides a seated view through the window beyond, while still affording the occupant overhead storage. *Courtesy of The HON Company*

Exposed beams add to the intimate, comfortable atmosphere of this office.
Courtesy of Lindal Cedar Homes

Establishing a corner for homework doesn't guarantee that a child will manage to ignore their playthings, but it helps. *Courtesy of Herman Miller, Inc.*

A corner workstation offers an expanse of surface space and ample under-counter storage. *Courtesy of Herman Miller, Inc.*

A stunning choice, black walls allow wicker and wood to leap out. Acrylic block windows add to the mystery and sense of solitude created by the dark surrounds. *Courtesy of Hy-Lite Products, Inc.*

A wallpaper border adds a bookshelf above modular office units. *Courtesy of Palliser® Furniture*

The work of design is best done within a well-designed environment. *Courtesy of Sligh Furniture Co.*

Against a Wall

Two wood tones add interest to a wall of flat-front cabinetry. *Courtesy of Lexington Home Brands*

A strip of countertop might double for a baking project, but it's generally set aside for the business work of the household. *Courtesy of Wellborn Cabinet, Inc.*

An office chair may be required to do double duty at the dining room table, in which case, style should be versatile. *Courtesy of Lexington Home Brands*

Relegation to a back wall doesn't necessarily imply a sacrifice in style. Here a single wall unit provides a complete office at home in any room. *Courtesy of Lexington Home Brands*

Below:
A ladies dressing room includes a work area, forming a lovely frame for a picture window. *Courtesy of Canac®*

Semi-transparent windows are reflected in two etched-glass cabinet fronts. *Courtesy of Palliser® Furniture*

Below:
Clients come to call in this home office, so visitors' chairs were provided. In setting up this office, the homeowner planned on making it a daylong place of work. *Courtesy of Merillat®*

Office Nooks

Desks aren't exclusively for writing and ciphering. Here the owner bends his back to the task of fly tying.
Courtesy of Jim Bishop Cabinets, Inc.

Utilizing a walk-through area to the kitchen, expense wasn't spared on this little nook office. Cream-colored custom cabinetry, recessed lighting, and glass shelving add up to lovely effect. *Courtesy of Harrison Design Associates*

A mirrored backsplash offers anyone seated at the desk a glance back at the kitchen behind. *Courtesy of Harrison Design Associates*

Handsome cabinetry turns an office area into a showplace. *Courtesy of Kemper Distinctive Cabinetry*

Custom cabinetry houses a wardrobe alongside a small workspace. *Design: Janice Thomas/Courtesy of Wood-Mode*

Below:
A pine desk tucked under the eaves enjoys regular patronage, offering a private space to place phone calls and keep up with correspondence. *Courtesy of Lindal Cedar Homes*

A small office center neatly contains all the accouterments of computer and fax machine.
Courtesy of Palliser® Furniture

Photographer Leonard Lammi

Built into what was once a closet under a stairway, the owners count this wee office as found space. There's more: under the desk is a lift-up floor that leads to a crawl space under the house. *Courtesy of Cross Interiors*

A thoroughly feminine backdrop highlights this vintage-style writing table and chair. *Courtesy of Ethan Allen, Inc.*

Talk about convenience – an office nook is located right next to a wet bar and warmed by a wood-stove. *Design: Janice Stone Thomas/Courtesy of Wood-Mode*

A kitchen office is stylishly integrated into a stunningly rich design by Barbara Ostrom. *Courtesy of Wood-Mode*

A bright, funky home office area makes for a fun place to pay bills or finish up other typically tedious chores. *Courtesy of Plain & Fancy*

A space-saving built-in desk features a pullout surface for the laptop, a flat, tuck-away stool, several storage drawers, and four apothecary-style cubbyholes. *Courtesy of Plain & Fancy*

Wrought iron provides a classic wall stand, in this case configured to act as home office. *Courtesy of Ethan Allen, Inc.*

Albeit small, a short stretch of counter proves useful for drafting letters and those monthly checks. *Courtesy of California Redwood Association*

Antique table and chair add unique flair to a home's corner office. *Courtesy of Bruce Hardwood Floors/The Hardwood Council*

French doors separate, and sometimes unite, kitchen and office area. *Courtesy of Congoleum Corp.*

Kitchens are where things get done, from three meals a day, to the bills that pay for them. *Courtesy of Harrison Design Associates*

Photo by Lynn McGill

Tile backsplash and cabinetry trim integrate a small office area with the rest of the kitchen. *Courtesy of Decorá*

The business is generally tucked into drawers and cabinets, convenient to a counter desktop. *Design: Dave Meyers/Courtesy of Wood-Mode*

A built-in bench allows two to confab over bills and other business matters in a kitchen office nook.
Design: Dan Parks/Courtesy of Wood-Mode

Minimalist

A glass-top desk on funky, Z-shaped supports opens the view and the atmosphere.
Courtesy of Topdeq

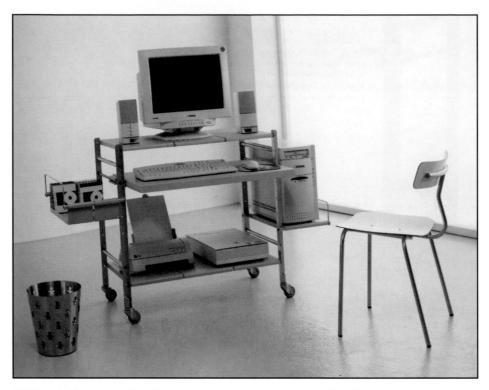

Defining simplicity and utility, this compact computer stand creates adjustable spaces for all your technology needs. *Courtesy of Bís Bís Imports Boston*

Efficient in function, this small corner unit is sufficient for the owner's needs.
Courtesy of The HON Company

Simple and inexpensive, wire
shelving was put to work, quite
literally, in this home office.
What's more – no dusting!
Courtesy of ClosetMaid

Two sleek tables and a matching
metallic and black bookcase make for
a modern, and mobile, home office
configuration. *Courtesy of Palliser®
Furniture*

A sleek desk adds to the clean and open effect of soaring walls and ceiling. *Courtesy of Lindal Cedar Homes*

With little ones, it's critical to keep documents and equipment tucked behind doors and in drawers. *Courtesy of Herman Miller, Inc.*

Flex Time

Sparse furnishings allow for a concentration on the view. A drafting table folds away when the work is done and exercise equipment wheels out to reconfigure the room's role at other times. *Courtesy of Simonton Windows*

Fold-away desks are the perfect solution when an office shares space with other living quarters.
Courtesy of Topdeq

Opposite page:
A cabinet opens to reveal a complete office. *Courtesy of Palliser® Furniture*

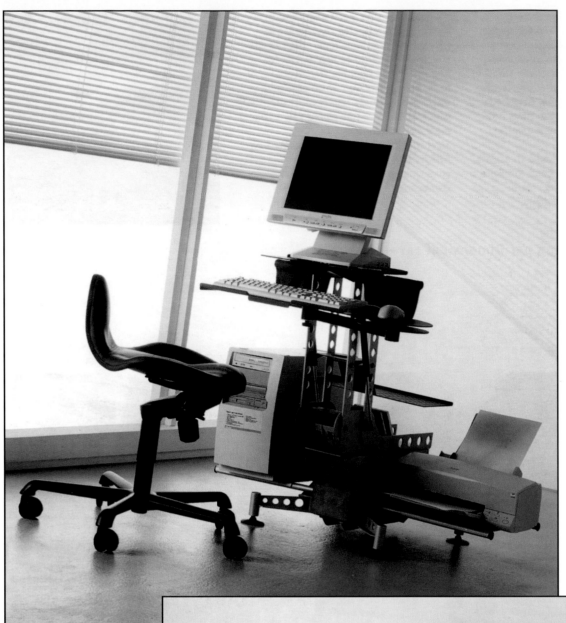

Innovative design allows computer monitor and keyboard to tuck away when not in use, or to come to attention. Adjustable designs create work environments for those who like to stand as well as sit. *Courtesy of Bis Bis Imports Boston*

A carved armoire is configured as computer cabinet, complete with pullout keyboard shelf, storage shelf, a locking file drawer, and an electrical outlet. *Courtesy of Ethan Allen, Inc.*

A mission-style chair gets wheels, combining utility with style to match the computer workstation. *Courtesy of Ethan Allen, Inc.*

A rollaway desk tucks under a long counter when not in use, opening the view to sliding glass doors.
Courtesy of California Redwood Association

Since you spend most of your time in the bedroom anyway, you might want to consider getting some work done there.
Courtesy of Ethan Allen, Inc.

Folding table and chair need not be flimsy. Indeed, these are often left standing in order to serve as a home office, but are easily tucked away for special occasions. *Courtesy of Lindal Cedar Homes*

A pedestal table serves for dining and, after the dishes are cleared, a spot where homework gets done.
Courtesy of Ethan Allen, Inc.

Sleek, utilitarian furnishings are perfect for their super techie owner. *Courtesy of The HON Company*

Conventional Workspaces

Honeyed tones were used in wood, wallpaper, and window treatments.
Courtesy of Knudson Gloss

Antiqued hardware and exotic allure combine. *Courtesy of Ethan Allen, Inc.*

Custom cabinetry allows for a long stretch of workspace in this U-shaped office, as well as three walls of shelving. *Courtesy of Charles Cabinet Co.*

Simple woodwork creates standout style in a white environment. *Courtesy of Palliser® Furniture*

Below:
An overstuffed leather chair adds executive ambiance to this home office. *Courtesy of Lexington Home Brands*

Shelves three deep cap this custom-made workstation. *Courtesy of Lindal Cedar Homes*

Right & opposing page:
Semi-custom built shelving and cabinets can easily be converted from office storage to household utility should the need arise. *Courtesy of KraftMaid Cabinetry*

Steel office furnishings may be standard fare, but they dress up nicely with art and accessories. *Courtesy of The HON Company*

Carpet is used to denote different uses within a large, open room. *Courtesy of The HON Company*

Custom cabinetry produces a sense of establishment. *Courtesy of Wood-Mode*

A framed sheet of currency serves as reminder of the true meaning of business. However, business is tucked away when it's family time. *Courtesy of Wood-Mode*

Semi-circular bookcases cap two ends of an L-shaped work area, adding style and accessibility.
Courtesy of The HON Company

A wrap-around desk forms a work shelter, providing a wealth of desktop for tasks.
Courtesy of The HON Company

Extensive filing cabinets create an archival system for an office that will be used for many years to come. *Courtesy of The HON Company*

Boxes and cylindrical containers help in the constant war on clutter. *Courtesy of Palliser® Furniture*

Modular units allow for easy reconfigurations of a work area. *Courtesy of Palliser® Furniture*

Two-tone furnishings – black cabinetry topped by natural wood tones, make a powerful statement in style. *Courtesy of The HON Company*

Mid-century appeal is embodied in this contemporary office. *Courtesy of Ethan Allen, Inc.*

Her office: for running the household, doing the bills, keeping up with the correspondence, and planning special events. *Courtesy of Harrison Design Associates*

A filing cabinet rolls under an unobtrusive bedroom desk unit. *Courtesy of Herman Miller, Inc.*

A U-shaped desk establishes a work area that capitalizes on the view, while not blocking it. *Courtesy of Herman Miller, Inc.*

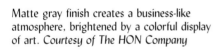

Matte gray finish creates a business-like atmosphere, brightened by a colorful display of art. *Courtesy of The HON Company*

Unconventional

Retractable shades filter light and create great checks of color in this lofty office space, furnished with an inspiring mix of plain and stunning contemporary pieces.
Courtesy of Lindal Cedar Homes

Created to curb back problems years ago, this oddly configured chair has won the heart of one occupant. *Courtesy of Lindal Cedar Homes*

Below:
The heavy stuff is stored around the perimeters, allowing mobile furnishings to be rotated according to the work at hand. *Courtesy of Topdeq*

A mahogany bookcase swings open to reveal the library powder room. The expert engineering prevents things from falling off the shelves during opening and closing. This is the most talked about feature of a wonderful new home. *Courtesy of Sroka Design, Inc.*

All Americana, this red, white, and blue room reflects a popular post 9-11 trend in home decor.
Courtesy of Ethan Allen, Inc.

Reclaimed Spaces

The business at hand here is cooking, sometimes requiring computers and books.
Courtesy of Harrison Design Associates

The space under a stairwell is put to work. *Courtesy of California Closets*

A basement work area includes computer workstations and a filing cabinet on wheels.
Courtesy of Palliser® Furniture

A lofty office commands a view of the entrance and allows the worker to keep and eye and ear on the household, too.
Courtesy of Yankee Barn Homes

A computer alcove was tucked into a stair landing, offering two a fantastic view as well as their own work port.
Courtesy of Knudson Gloss

A lofty nook lends itself to the sense of distance one needs from the comforts of home when serious work is afoot.
Courtesy of Wood-Mode

Tucked under the eaves, a lofty work retreat is lined with wonderful custom cabinetry and matching woodwork.
Courtesy of Wood-Mode

A loft apartment is divided by half walls, allowing communication, and sunlight to permeate throughout. *Courtesy of The HON Company*

A bookcase tucks under windows in this converted attic, furnished in contemporary blond tones. *Courtesy of Ethan Allen, Inc.*

A sportsman's retreat affords a place to unwind while tying flies for fishing. *Courtesy of Yankee Barn Homes*

©Brad Simmons

A basement office is stylishly lit by square transom windows, mimicked in the lines of cabinetry and artwork.
Courtesy of The HON Company

Below:
A small space feels more open when clean lines are maintained, accomplished here using sleek white facing and a faux granite countertop.
Courtesy of California Closets

A full-service, efficient space includes adjustable shelving and a correspondence area where stationary and smaller items are kept within arm's reach. *Courtesy of California Closets*

Modular furnishings allow an office designer to configure to the existing space. *Courtesy of Sligh Furniture Co.*

Reclaimed industrial space is increasingly popular in real estate-poor cities. Here, handsome furnishings add elegance to the rough textures of a former life. *Courtesy of Sligh Furniture Co.*

Family Affairs

No one family member can lay claim to this multi-function area – mom does her crafts and sewing, dad gets online to check email, and junior may undertake a coloring project. *Courtesy of California Closets*

Modular furniture helps make the most of limited space in a child's room, though ample space was allotted for homework. *Courtesy of Lindal Cedar Homes*

Wood and rattan team up in this stylish, one-wall office where two might work side-by-side. *Courtesy of Wood-Mode*

Part of a floor-to-ceiling island area between kitchen and living areas, this desk was neatly incorporated. *Courtesy of Decorá*

Sentiment and old-fashioned style are reflected in a desk, chair, and barrister bookcase that might have been manufactured seventy years ago, but are as new as the home they adorn. *Courtesy of Lexington Home Brands*

Two can work as one, with side-by-side desk areas that serve the business needs of an entire family.
Courtesy of California Closets

Dad was hoping for company when he built his home office. A padded bench encourages family members to drop by for a chat. *Courtesy of Sligh Furniture Co.*

Besides the dry business of paperwork and digital transactions, a desk is also a place where we snack, drink, and drum our fingers. Therefore, it's important to consider the durability of a desk surface when choosing office furnishings. *Courtesy of DuPont Corian®*

Making your child's room a great escape involves furnishings that suit his or her needs, from chairs to read in and a desk for homework, to innovative storage spaces and sleeping systems. *Courtesy of Ethan Allen, Inc.*

A chalkboard table, stacking crates, and a kid-sized bookshelf create a perfect corner office for a toddler. *Courtesy of Offi*

Executive Suites

Classic capitals characterize an office fashioned from custom cabinetry.
Courtesy of Wood-Mode

An enormous expanse of desk space is even more impressive when left uncluttered. Storage in desk drawers, a sideboard, and barrister bookcase allow for the impressive view. *Courtesy of Lexington Home Brands*

A second-floor office commands an impressive view. Wood furnishings were chosen to coordinate with wood ceiling and window trim in this lofty retreat. *Courtesy of Lexington Home Brands*

An executive office set features an English saddle leather desktop and hardwood solids and veneers.
Courtesy of Sligh Furniture Co.

Paneled floor to ceiling, complete with chandelier, this room creates a classic seat of power for the lord of the manor.
Courtesy of Harrison Design Associates

Thick curtains pull closed and a gas fire leaps to life, making a warm space even more intimate on demand. *Courtesy of Harrison Design Associates*

A wall of books provides a research staple for this handsomely appointed home office. *Courtesy of Harrison Design Associates*

Olive drab is an enduring color in interior design, creating a warm atmosphere for work or play. *Courtesy of Ethan Allen, Inc.*

When designing an office at home, first assess how much writing surface, shelving, filing, and computer space you will require. *Courtesy of Ethan Allen, Inc.*

A private office occupies a front room of the home, allowing visitors to stop in without disturbing the rest of the household. A wet bar is adjacent. *Courtesy of Decorá*

Opposite page:
An office acts as central command center. Seated under an overhang for privacy, the owner can hear all that transpires around her. *Courtesy of National Custom Homes*

The mere addition of black accessories and a stylish carpet adds contemporary flair to an impressive collection of matching office furnishings. A different carpet and accessories would quickly alter the entire look. *Courtesy of The HON Company*

Lovingly polished woof furnishings reflect the sleek city lights, as well as the owner's pride. *Courtesy of The HON Company*

The owner's collection of rare weaponry inspired the rug design, an intriguing presentation in this private office. *Courtesy of Soroush Custom Rugs & Axminster Carpet*

A private study faces a back lawn, creating a space to escape for contemplation. *Courtesy of Simonton Windows*

Below:
A classic, stuffed leather chair, black desktop, and custom cabinetry combine for a sense of establishment. *Courtesy of KraftMaid Cabinetry/The Hurdwood Council*

An oval desk top adds classic international style to a one-wall office unit. *Courtesy of Halcon*

Lest some family member forget and barge into the sanctum, this spacious retreat is labeled office, its boundaries sacred. *Courtesy of Yankee Barn Homes*

A custom-built desk matches the cabinetry for an impressive display. *Courtesy of Layline*

Adjacent to the dining room, this handsome office invites after-dinner conversation, where business can be discussed within the casual, friendly atmosphere of the home. *Courtesy of The HON Company*

Work becomes a luxury in a room with such appointments, particularly the expansive bow windows.
Courtesy of Sligh Furniture Co.

Staying Connected

In an open area of the home, this office serves the needs of all the family members, from homework to bills to vacation planning. *Courtesy of Harrison Design Associates*

An initial adds a personal touch to a custom desk. *Courtesy of Lindal Cedar Homes*

A home office was established using a tabletop to span the distance between two walls. Stacking drawers and open shelving create practical, attractive storage, and a Lafonda chair adds a central style statement. *Courtesy of Herman Miller, Inc.*

A bow-shaped desk culminates in a display easel, where the dictionary and other research materials are an arm's-length away.
Courtesy of Herman Miller, Inc.

Incorporating your personal style is one of the motivating and enriching aspects of appointing your own office.
Courtesy of Sligh Furniture Co.

An adjacent table invites retreat from the desk, and a fresh perspective on the work at hand.
Courtesy of The HON Company

Facing a desk into the room forces a sense of focus, while also adding natural light to the work at hand. *Courtesy of Congoleum Corp.*

A carpet separates work and leisure space, the office left open to communicate with living areas of the home. *Courtesy of Knudson Gloss*

Dedicated to work, this room doesn't exclude other family members. Rather, it provides places where multiple people can concentrate while in each other's company. *Courtesy of Lindal Cedar Homes*

Locked Retreat

You pay for the view, why not arrange your furniture to best enjoy it?
Courtesy of Simonton Windows

A wall of finished log characterizes this wonderful office, set off from the rest of the home by French doors.
Courtesy of Lindal Cedar Homes

A marble fireplace surround creates perfect contrast with wood paneling. *Courtesy of Harrison Design Associates*

Rich finish in an artfully paneled room adds formal grace to this private den.
Courtesy of Harrison Design Associates

A library/office is the perfect place for that serious talk, be it a family meeting, or a business aside following a social dinner.
Courtesy of Wood-Mode

Newsprint makes an interesting wallpaper in a room dedicated to reading. *Courtesy of Harrison Design Associates*

A writing desk tucks away in a hunter's trophy room. *Courtesy of Harrison Design Associates*

A drop leaf extends the work area in this classically appointed office, which includes a dust-proof barrister bookcase. *Courtesy of Ethan Allen, Inc.*

A spare bedroom is used for office work, commanding a stylish, soaring space. *Courtesy of KraftMaid Cabinetry*

Semi-custom cabinetry and furnishings make this office part of the home when not in use for business. *Courtesy of KraftMaid Cabinetry*

A dream room for someone who works at home, this one includes a view and an executive's share of storage and shelving. *Courtesy of Wood-Mode*

A coffee table mimics leather-bound books, adding a unique dimension to this inviting, intimate den. *Courtesy of Harrison Design Associates*

A classic, masculine retreat, perfectly stocked and appointed. *Courtesy of Harrison Design Associates*

Cameron Wood Photography

White cabinetry works with room trim in contrast to blue wallpaper. *Design: Ronald G. Cook/Courtesy of Wood-Mode*

Zebra stripes, pottery, and other accents add exotic atmosphere to a room rich with traditional paneling features. *Courtesy of Knudson Gloss*

A desk commands the business end of a long room, customized with wall-to-wall paneling and built-in shelves.
Courtesy of Wood-Mode and the Hardwood Council

A skyline view makes the office one of this apartment's most attractive rooms. *Courtesy of Herman Miller, Inc.*

A small room takes on a big role, serving both as home office and a central storage area.
Courtesy of Wellborn Cabinet, Inc.

Peach tones add tropical flair to this feminine office setting. *Courtesy of Ethan Allen, Inc.*

Contemporary

A keyhole-shaped, retractable desktop, frosted glass cabinets, and an artful backdrop make a fashion statement for the owner. *Courtesy of Steelcase, Inc.*

Two wooden filing cabinets act as stylish base to a contemporary desk. *Courtesy of Bruce Hardwood Floors/The Hardwood Council*

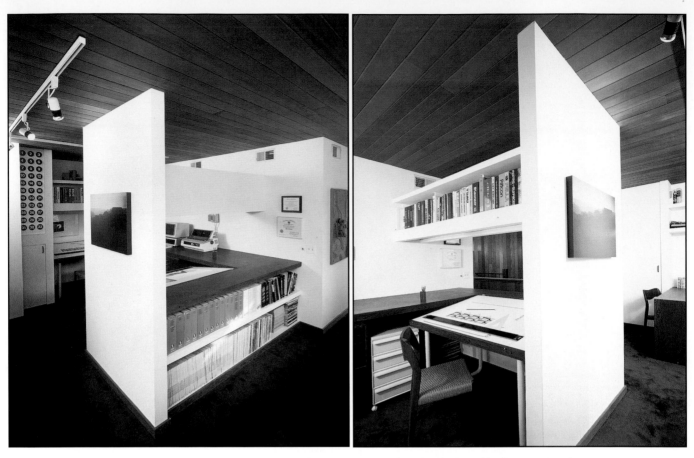

A home work area is clearly demarcated, though left open on two sides. A need for lots of book, manual, and magazine storage is met with under counter storage and a suspended shelf. *Courtesy of California Redwood Association*

Bold strokes of color characterize this work space, shared with eating areas and an adjacent kitchen.
Courtesy of Topdeq

A computer station rolls on casters to the site most convenient to the occupant. *Courtesy of Topdeq*

Sleek black countertop and cabinetry with chrome accents create contemporary flair in a highly-functional office space. *Courtesy of Wood-Mode*

A desk curves out from an artfully lit wall unit, with a file drawer on casters to extend the arc even further.
Courtesy of Halcon

Custom glass inserts adorn cabinetry, creating a space with style. *Courtesy of Meríllat®*

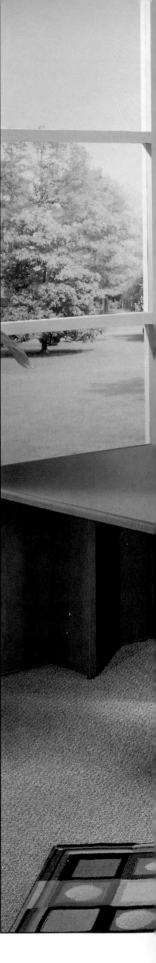

Purple walls, a polka-dot carpet, and framed art spice up a clean-cut office ensemble.
Courtesy of The HON Company

Four artfully framed photographs create a geometric backsplash between symmetrical cabinets. *Courtesy of Decorá*

Art Deco styling is characterized in clean lines and the simple elegance of the details. *Courtesy of Lexington Home Brands*

A half wall offers auditory access to the family's rooms beyond.
Courtesy of The HON Company.

Animals and outstanding red accents characterize a home office, furnished with contemporary pieces, including a three-tier, tuck-away desk.
Courtesy of Herman Miller, Inc.

Classic, simple, and elegant furnishings make a distinctive workplace.
Courtesy of Ethan Allen, Inc.

Modular paneling with cubbyholes forms a creative backdrop in this functional office setting.
Courtesy of The HON Company

Nostalgic appeal is created with clean lines and two-tone chair, recalling Art Deco styling of the 1930s. *Courtesy of Ethan Allen, Inc.*

Photography by Scott Frances and Tria Giovan

Black and white furnishings add Art Deco flair to a paneled office. *Courtesy of Harrison Design Associates*

Opposite page:
Blond paneling is the perfect compliment to a room rich in both windows and wood tones. *Courtesy of Sroka Design, Inc.*

A well-designed home office over the garage makes it possible for the homeowner to telecommute. *Courtesy of Sroka Design, Inc.*

Style is expressed in a simple collection of metallic desk ornaments and plain book covers.
The result is a simple corner office that stays tidy by design. *Courtesy of Palliser® Furniture*

A circular extension adds style and workspace, easily accessible from different angles, or for an impromptu meeting.
Courtesy of The HON Company

Albeit all egg-white, delicate touches in the furnishings identify the femininity of the owner. *Courtesy of Harrison Design Associates*

Photo by Lynn McGill

Who says an office chair has to swivel and roll?
Comfort and style are important considerations, too.
Courtesy of Ethan Allen, Inc.

Below:
Yellow adds warmth on the walls, and upholstery provides a
splash of color to a wood-rich office setting. *Courtesy of
The HON Company*

Tables and lounge chair of classic Eames design turn this spare room into a stylish office retreat.
Courtesy of Herman Miller, Inc.

Purple walls and an oval window are bold accompaniments to a contemporary kitchen-corner office. *Courtesy of Herman Miller, Inc.*

A table on wheels acts as mobile desk, rolling between the confines of matching office furnishings.
Courtesy of Steelcase, Inc.

Standard office equipment in the home enhances storage for household goods as well as the effects of business.
Courtesy of The HON Company

A comfy chair is key to inducing extended work hours. *Courtesy of Palliser® Furniture*

Projected artwork on black walls, and burl-wood veneer on office furnishings, create a unique statement in this work environment. *Courtesy of Steelcase, Inc.*

Blond cabinetry conceals office clutter, while multi-level work areas encourage a healthy mix of sitting and standing. *Courtesy of Steelcase, Inc.*

Classic Studies

A den is open to a lofty walkway, with the book theme continuing on the second floor.
Courtesy of Harrison Design Associates

Pearson Photography, Annapolis, MD

This condo library incorporates the look of another century, with the surprise of technology hidden behind the pilaster to bring in creature comforts of modern-day living. *Courtesy of Sroka Design, Inc.*

Below:
Burl-wood paneling from floor to ceiling, dark leather furnishings, and subtle lighting add to the serious atmosphere of this home office. *Courtesy of Harrison Design Associates*

Photo by Robert Thien

A warm fire, an ancestral portrait, leather seating, custom woodwork — all elements that add up to a sense of timelessness in this wonderful library room. *Design: Helen Marshburn/Courtesy of Wood-Mode*

Who wouldn't want this desk? And so simple — a table offers window-side seating with an attractive view of the fire. *Courtesy of Harrison Design Associates*

Light wood paneling and upholstered furnishings create a classic yet comfortable den for work or gatherings. *Courtesy of Harrison Design Associates*

Hand-carved woodwork, art, and precious family images add up to opulence in this home office environment. *Courtesy of Weinstein Design Group*

Royal blue carpet underfoot and formal family portraits add gentrified air to this stately office/library. *Courtesy of Lindal Cedar Homes*

Below:
Tonal woods and red meld for rich, warm effect in this fire-lit office retreat. *Courtesy of Addison Development*

Kim Sargent, Palm Beach Gardens, FL

Spotlights in the ceiling panels supplement shaded lamps, for glowing effect in a room both inviting and impressive. *Courtesy of Harrison Design Associates*

Gil Stose Photography

Comfortable seating and stacks of reading material are draws in this home library. *Courtesy of Wood-Mode*

This new pine library in a renovated 1906 home looks as if it has always been part of the house. *Courtesy of Sroka Design, Inc.*

Marble, leather, and custom paneling characterize a very masculine office. *Courtesy of Knudson Gloss*

Custom paneling fills an office floor to ceiling, creating old world elegance in a new home. *Courtesy of Knudson Gloss*

An antique desk provides a warm and inviting place to work in this penthouse library. *Courtesy of Sroka Design, Inc.*

Pearson Photography, Annapolis, MD

Glass cabinetry reduces the need for dusting in a richly-paneled office library. *Courtesy of Wood-Mode*

A study isn't just for books. In this case, homework involves practice at the piano. *Courtesy of Congoleum Corp.*

135

All About Books

Recessed lighting and a ladder on a rail give the impression of greater height in this library room. *Courtesy of Charles Cabinet Co.*

Royal blue carpet underfoot and formal family portraits add gentrified air to this stately office/library. *Courtesy of Lindal Cedar Homes*

Dining rooms double as libraries, perfect for people who like to discuss good books over dinner. *Courtesy of Wood-Mode*

A dream reading room, this one offers a comfortable chair where one can become established amidst a flush of tree-filtered light, surrounded on three sides by good books. *Courtesy of Pella Windows*

A perfect place to gather for tales following the foxhunt. *Courtesy of Harrison Design Associates*

Family images compete for shelf space with the reading material in this handsome den. *Courtesy of Charles Cabinet Co.*

A home library spans two stories, stacked with books. *Design: Thomas D. Kling/Courtesy of Wood-Mode*

An office area is attached visually with a living area and library beyond. *Courtesy of Wood-Mode*

Leather chairs furnish a classic library retreat.
Courtesy of The HON Company

Sandwiched between bookshelves, a beautiful table offers a work surface for a frequent researcher. *Courtesy of Knudson Gloss*

A simple table desk receives backup assistance from a wall of shelves. *Courtesy of the Hardwood Manufacturers Association and the Hardwood Council*

Opposite page:
A spiral staircase bridges the distance between desk and a reference library.
Courtesy of National Custom Homes/ Brantley Photography, Delray Beach, FL

Exposed beams, a window-studded bow, and an impressive wall of books make an unforgettable impression. *Courtesy of Knudson Gloss*

Below:
A fireplace warms the area below the eaves, with woodwork to match the impressive stretch of library that circles the room. *Courtesy of Knudson Gloss*

Resource Guide

Addison Development
215 Fifth Street, Suite 100
West Palm Beach, FL 33401
561-802-4411

Bis Bis Imports Boston
4 Park Plaza
Boston, MA 02116
617-350-7565
www.bisbis.com

California Closets
1000 Fourth Street, Suite 800
San Rafael, CA 94901
800-274-6754
www.calclosets.com

California Redwood Association
405 Enfrente Drive, Suite 200
Novato, CA 94949
415-382-0662
www.calredwood.org

Canac Kitchens
360 John Street
Thornhill, Ontario L3T 3M9 Canada
905-881-9725
www.canackitchens.com

Charles Cabinet Co.
3090 N. Cleveland avenue
Roseville, MN 55113
651-633-1488
www.charlescabinetco.com

ClosetMaid
PO Box 4400
Ocala, FL 34478
800-221-0641
www.closetmaid.com

Congoleum Corp.
3500 Quakerbridge Road
Mercerville, NJ 08619-0127
800-274-3266
www.congoleum.com

Cross Interiors
6712 Colbath Avenue
Van Nuys, CA 91405
818-988-2047
www.crossinteriors.com

Decorá
One MasterBrand Cabinets Drive
Jasper, IN 47546
812-482-2527
www.mbcabinets.com

DuPont Corian®
P.O. Box 80012
Barley Mill Plaza — Building 12
Wilmington, DE 19880-0012
1-800-426-7426
www.corian.com

Ethan Allen, Inc.
Ethan Allen Drive, PO Box 1966
Danbury, CT 06813
203-743-8000
www.ethanallen.com

Halcon, A Teknion Company
1811 Second Avenue NEW
Stewartville, MN 55876
507-533-4235
www.halconcorp.com

The Hardwood Council
PO Box 525
Oakmont, PA 15139
412-281-4980
www.hardwoodcouncil.com

Harrison Design Associates
3198 Cains Hill Place, NW Suite 200
Atlanta, GA 30305
404-365-7760
www.Harrisondesignassociates.com

Herman Miller, Inc.
PO Box 302
Zeeland, MI 49464
888-443-4357
www.hermanmiller.com

The HON Company
200 Oak Street
Muscatine, Iowa 52761
Phone: 800-624-9212
www.hon.com

Hy-Lite Products, Inc.
101 California Avenue
Beaumont, CA 92223
877-712-4013
www.hy-lite.com

Jim Bishop Cabinets, Inc.
P.O. Box 11424
Montgomery, AL 36111
800-410-2444, ext. 3017
www.jimbishopcabinets.com

KraftMaid Cabinetry
PO Box 1055
Middlefield, OH 44062
800-571-1990
www.kraftmaid.com

Lay Line Projects
3521 Commodore Circle
Delray Beach, FL 33483.
Phone: 954-709-1755

Lexington Home Brands
PO Box 1008
Lexington NC 27293-1008
800-539-4636
www.lexington.com

Lindal Cedar Homes
4300 South 104th Place
Seattle, WA 98178
206-725-0900
www.lindal.com

Kemper Distinctive Cabinetry
One MasterBrand Cabinets Drive
Jasper, IN 47546
812-482-2527
www.mbcabinets.com

Knudson Gloss Architects Planners
4820 Riverbend Road
Boulder, CO 80301
303-442-5882
www.kgarch.com

Merillat®
PO Box 1946
Adrian, MI 49221
800-575-8763
www.merrillat.com

National Custom Homes
15415 Mizner Club Drive
Boca Raton, FL 33446
561-495-0309
www.nationalcustomhomes.com

Offi
5850 Hollis Street
Emeryville, CA 94608
800-383-6334
www.offi.com

Palliser® Furniture, Ltd.
70 Lexington Park
Winnipeg, MB
Canada R2G 4H2
204-988-3398
www.palliser.com

Pella Corporation
102 Main Street
Pella, IA 50219
515-628-1000
www.pella.com

Plain & Fancy Custom Cabinetry
Route 501 & Oak Street
P.O. Box 519
Schaefferstown, PA 17088
800-447-9006
www.plainfancycabinetry.com

Progress Lighting
PO Box 5704
Spartanburg, SC 29304
864-599-6000
www.progresslighting.com

Simonton Windows
P.O. Box 1646
Parkersburg, WV 26102
800-746-6686
www.simonton.com

Sligh Furniture Co.
1201 Industrial Avenue
Holland, MI 49423
616-392-7101
www.sligh.com

Soroush Custom Rugs & Axminster Carpet
10400 Connecticut Ave., 1st Floor
Kensington, MD 20895
301-929-5000
www.soroushcustomrugs.com

Sroka Design, Inc.
7307 Macarthur Blvd., Suite 214
Bethesda, MD 20816
301-263-9100
www.srokadesign.com

Steelcase Furniture Co.
PO Box 1967
Grand Rapids, MI 49501
www.steelcase.com

Topdeq
3 Security Drive #303
Cranbury, NJ 08512
866-876-3300
www.topdeq.com

Weinstein Design Group
902 Clint Moore Road, Suite 218
Boca Raton, FL 33446
561-997-6770
www.weinsteindesigngroup.com

Wellborn Cabinet, Inc.
38669 Highway 77
Ashland, AL 36251
256-354-7022
www.wellborncabinet.com

Wood-Mode Fine Custom Cabinetry
One Second Street
Kreamer, PA 17833
570-374-2711
www.wood-mode-com

Yankee Barn Homes
131 Yankee Barn Road
Grantham, NH 03753
603-863-4545
www.yankeebarnhomes.com